HOW TO SAVE YOUR

MARRIAGE

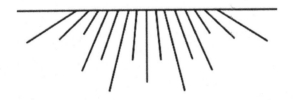

100 Ways to Turn

your Broken Relationship into a

Happy Marriage

By Sarah Mitchell

Table of Contents

How Did I Get Here?

That's what you're thinking, isn't it?

How did you get to the point where you're buying a book entitled "How to Save your Marriage?"

It's a scary place to be in. But take comfort in knowing that you won't be in that scary place for long.

If you're here at the first sign of trouble, that shows great commitment and incredible dedication to the health of your relationship.

And if you're here because you fear that your relationship is nearing divorce, the single fact that you are reading this book means that you are a fighter and that your love is worth fighting for.

You're not alone. In fact, you're in constant company.

So much so, that there exists years of research and decades of studies dedicated to the success and creation of happy marriages, that teach experts and couples how to revive even the most lifeless, sexless, and seemingly loveless marriage.

This book is a harmoniously balanced collection of those studies – that when combined- create the most beautiful storm that will not only fix your broken marriage, but also liven up parts of your marriage that you didn't even know were missing.

Before we dive into the good stuff, let's touch on the complicated stuff. Don't worry, this won't hurt a bit...

Why Do Marriages Fail?

When you start a new job- let's say as a truck driver of a massively powerful 18-wheeler, you don't just jump in the drivers seat and put the pedal to the metal. Why? Because you'd crash straight away.

The same *should* go for marriage. It's a job. It's an 18-wheeler carrying heavy cargo. Yet, we are all handed the keys and are allowed to jump in the drivers seat with absolutely no training on how to drive the marriage truck! It's no wonder we run over each others hearts and spill our responsibility all over the proverbial highway.

So, imagine that your relationship is an 18-wheeler and each wheel represents an element of marriage: Trust, Loyalty, Romance, Fun, Friendship, Finances, Parenthood....you get the picture.

Every wheel must be in shape for the truck to drive smoothly. There needs to be a balance between all parts.

The same goes for your relationship. You must tend to each area of your relationship for it to drive smoothly. And this book will help you do that.

This book is your driver's training manual. Each chapter will help you focus on a specific wheel to realign your marriage. Some wheels are flat, some are fine, and some don't even exist yet.

Whether you've totaled your relationship or you're just doing some proactive maintenance (good for you), by the end of this book, your marriage will be stronger than ever.

Oh, and two mechanics are always better than one. The methods in this book are meant to be shared with your partner.

If you'd like to get a grasp on these marriage-saving methods on your own first, go for it. Half of these methods you can apply by yourself. But when you're comfortable, share this book with your spouse. Read it together. Learn as a team.

Don't let the title of the book hold you back or make you afraid to tell your partner that you are so committed to your lifelong partnership, that you sought expert advice.

Plus, there are a few spicy chapters in here that no partner will be disappointed to find (wink wink).

So, get your highlighter ready. You'll need to read and reread each and every one of these steps until they become engrained in your daily relationship habits.

And once they do, you'll be so far from the path of divorce and back on the road to a fulfilling life full of love, memories, and a playful partnership.

Get your highlighter ready! Here we go!

Chapter 1: Friendship

Without a solid friendship as foundation, marriages have nothing to fall back on when money gets tight, sex gets put on the back burner, and kids overtake your household! At the end of the day, you and your partner must prioritize that bond.

Study after study backs up this philosophy. Take relationship expert John Gottman, professor at the University of Washington. In his studies, he has found that "Happy marriages are based on a deep friendship". He has also concluded that this friendship also serves as the bridge to romantic and physical satisfaction.

Couples who prioritize that friendship have higher success rates in their marriage and report higher rates of martial satisfaction. Why? Because who doesn't want to hang out with their best friend forever and ever?

So, how do we go from feeling like strangers, or even perhaps enemies, to friends? We start over and build.

Here are proven friendship building activities and techniques that can restore that foundation in your marriage.

1. Be on the Same Team

Once you're married, you're on the same team forever, every day, til death do you part.

Recognize that you have the same goals. Realize that what is good for your partner is good for you. Encourage your partner to reach for their goals. Motivate your partner to push through tough times. You are your partner's coach and teammate.

And just like in every sport every played, you never turn your back on your partner, deceive them, or wish for them to fail. Because when they fail, you fail.

2. Revive your Shared Common Interests

Think back to when you and your partner first met. What was it that you both enjoyed doing together? What were the commonalities that drew the 2 of you together?

From your love for the outdoors to your enthusiasm for dive bars- take this little ember and bring it back to life!

By weaving shared interests back into your coupled routine, you begin to associate positive feelings with spending time with your partner.

Can't figure out any common interests? Easy solution.

Discover a new common interest by taking some online quizzes. Search "Shared Common Interests" online. Yes, this may seem cheesy but you're both going to have to put your ego aside and really dive into this process.

3. Celebrate Successes Big and Small

When you get married, you take on the role of being your partner's biggest cheerleader and #1 fan. Remember that we are all just big kids inside and we want to feel like our loved one is proud of us.

Hang that Employee of the Month Certificate on the fridge, take them out to ice cream to celebrate their promotion, buy them a new outfit to make a good impression when they start that new job, and take them to dinner when they've finished a jig saw puzzle because why not?! Life should be full of celebrations!

Your spouse must always be able to count on you to lift them up and cheer them on.

4. Daily Download

For the first 10 minutes that your partner gets home, no phones or computers are allowed. Immediately sit down, engage in some physical touch and download everything that happened during each other's day.

This consistent pow wow will ensure that YOU are your partner's confidant and that you are up to speed on everything that is happening in your partners life, and visa versa. This is a sure fire way to build a solid friendship.

5. Make a Bucket List Together

Get crafty with stickers, sturdy stock paper, a ruler and fancy pens. You're about to make the bucket list of a lifetime! Take a trip to Japan, learn how to play tennis, go sky diving, get matching tattoos – and then commit to how many activities you're going to cross off the list per year. And remember, you're married...you have your whole life to complete this list! Don't hold back, kids.

6. Create Traditions

Unbreakable. Traditions are a metaphor for your relationship. They are promises that turn into sentimental memories that only the two of you share. Here are some ideas for shared traditions that you can start ASAP.

❖ Weekly Traditions

✓ Meet for lunch every Wednesday

✓ Every night before bed, do a countdown of the "Top 10 Best Things That Happened Today" – alternating turns.

✓ Go on a walk together every evening or walk the dog together every morning

✓ Movie Night once a week – take turns picking the movie and the food

✓ Say a dinner blessing before you eat – it doesn't have to be religious! "Dear food, we love you and we're going to eat you now".

❖ Yearly Traditions

✓ Every holiday season, buy a new Christmas Tree Ornament or Holiday decoration together

- ✓ Have a pumpkin Carving Contest
- ✓ Craft elaborate Birthday Card's for each other
- ✓ Join a yearly marathon and train together
- ✓ Have a baking contest with your family as the judges

7. Try New Things Together

Go to the aquarium, try roller skating, learn how to snowboard, or just visit a new area of town and walk around!

Since the dawn of time, research shows that couples who try new things together share a stronger bond. Take the study by Arthur Aron, a professor of psychology at Stony Brook University. His study took 53 married couple and split them into 2. Half of the couples were challenged to trying new activities together, ones that were outside of their comfort zone and pushed them to rely on each other. The other half were assigned to do comfortable activities like going to the movies. They were to perform these tasks for only 90 minutes per week.

At the end of the 10- week study, the couples who tried new activities together reported a much higher marital satisfaction. Just after 10 weeks!

Pro Tip: Every city or town has an event calendar that includes beer festivals, music performances and volunteer opportunities. Start picking some organized activities and throw yourselves into the mix.

8. Ask your Partner to Teach you Something

What is a hobby or task that your spouse is good at but you have no knowledge about? How to ride a skateboard? How to make homemade pasta? Give your lover the chance to take the reins. Let them lead and be happy to follow. Watch how brightly they shine and how kind they can be.

9. Challenge Each Other on Game Apps

Your goal right now is to glue you and your partner back together. To do that, you need a fun and flirty activity that is going to keep you in contact throughout the day.

Download a game app on your phone and play intermittently while at work or on the go...

- ✓ **Chess**
- ✓ **Trivia**
- ✓ **Scrabble**
- ✓ **DuoLingo**

Just remember, keep it light and keep your competitive side in check.

10. Create your own Mini Book Club or Podcast Club

Download a podcast or book on tape and listen to it in the car on your commute. Make sure it's something you both have a vague interest in...otherwise your partner might not be too keen on listening to an hour of "Bee Keeping 101".

This is an easy way to create conversational material, help the two of you grow together and possibly align your interests to create an even deeper friendship.

11.   Plan a Vacation

Maybe it's not the right time to go on vacation, but creating an exciting get away in the next 6 months is something the 2 of you can look forward to together!

Pick a place near or far. Do a little research and plan a budget
Put the date on the calendar and request that time off. Then start saving!

Or if a vacation is totally impossible- plan a 'stay-cation' in your respective towns while you Periscope your day together

12.   Support their Dreams

Does your husband want to be an actor? Sign him up for a community theatre production and encourage him to go for it. Has your wife expressed her dream of one day becoming a cheese maker? Go online and buy her a cheese making kit- just because!

This love and support will mean the world to your partner, showing them that you listen and have their back.

Chapter 2: Intimacy

13.   Fall in Love Again

Sex and intimacy come easier when feelings are involved.

A famous relationship study by psychologist Arthur Aron at Stony Brook University has gone viral. It claimed that 36 simple questions asked and answered between 2 strangers, with the addition of 4- minutes of eye contact could make 2 strangers fall in love. And guess what...this study has plenty of success stories.

There are 3 sets of questions, each set growing increasingly more intimate that the last. Partners take turn asking the questions, with the partner who asked the question answering first. At the end of the 36 intense questions, you stare into each other's eyes for 4 minutes straight.

You'll need water, snacks, and a cozy place to sit. Dedicate as much time as you need to this exercise as it could very well put the two of you back on track.

14.   Stare into Each Other's Eyes

Keep up the connectivity practice once per week with some intimate eye contact.

According to a Japanese study that wired peoples brains with MRI mapping, staring into your partner's eyes for 4 minutes straight synchs up your brain activity to literally function with the same patterns. Think of this as mutual meditation.

Not only will this help you 2 connect on a physiological level, but the act of looking into someone else's eyes with no talking or distractions is extremely intimate and vulnerable. Try this once per week.

15. PDA

Public displays of affection let your partner know that you are proud to be by their side. Hold your partners hand, give them a sweet kiss, and put your arm around them. This also can make them feel protected and secure in new situations, letting them know that you are a team.

Tailor your levels of PDA to whatever feels natural to you, but don't neglect this opportunity that speaks volumes to how you feel about your partner.

16.   Give Massages

Human touch. We all need it. Especially from our partners.

After a study on 19 couples who massaged each other, the lead researcher Sayuri Naruse of Northumbria University said that massage is a "simple and effective way for couples to improve their physical and mental wellbeing whilst showing affection for one another,"

The most interesting finding of this study? Not only did the person receiving the massage feel more relaxed, but so did the person giving the massage. That's because sensual and intimate massages actually synch your breathing to your partner. You become one.

To ensure massage time every week, each partner gets a massage coupon from the other. Use oils and candles for a sexy massage or cash in your coupon in front of the TV.

17.   Cuddle Time

When couples cuddle, oxytocin or "the love hormone" is released. You start to find a safe place in your partner's arms. Pillow talk unveils vulnerabilities. And sometimes, cuddling leads to sex.

All of the above contribute to a deep level of intimacy that you share with no other human on this earth other than your spouse. It's an extremely special activity.

Mandatory Minimum: 5 minutes of fully embraced cuddling per day.

Chapter 3: Sexy Time

Sexual intimacy in a marriage is a key factor in marriage satisfaction on 2 levels.

The first is that sexually active people are happier (and less stressed) than non-sexually active people. Period. Therefore, when couples have sex together, it creates 2 happy people and 2 happy people can contribute to 1 happy marriage.

The second being that sex strengthens the bond between 2 people. It promotes trust and expression while releasing nostalgic hormones such as oxytocin and dopamine – all of which reignite that "spark".

Your relationship cannot survive without sexual intimacy, so here's what you're going to do.

5 days per week, there must be a sexual or intimate encounter of some kind. "Sexual Encounter" doesn't always mean 45 minutes of dedicated bedroom time. It could be a quick tease before work, an afternoon favor, an intimate cuddle, or yes...a full blown night of sexual fantasies.

Never the less, sexuality and intimacy are the glue that fuse friends into lovers.

18. Sext During the Day

A sexy photo or a racy message will get their heart pumping and down stairs tingling – especially when it's been quite a while since sexting went down.

Tell your partner what you want to do to them when they get home. Or send a photo of a new sex toy or piece of lingerie that you bought...on a Tuesday.

You're partner will be home faster than you can say "Do me".

19. Sex Dice

Kiss neck. Slap butt. Lick ear. Each roll of the dice comes up with some sensual combination that will make both of you tingle all over. For an extra tease, roll these dice right before you leave the house for work. Your partner will be dying to get home to you at the end of the day to finish what you've started.

20.   Fantasy Box

Convert an old tissue box into the Fantasy Box. Each of you writes at least 5 sexual fantasies on a piece of paper and places it in the box. A couple times per week, you take turns picking one slip of paper out of the box and acting out that sexual fantasy no matter what.

Be sure to keep refilling the box. This will keep your mind wandering and your thirst for your partner's body alive.

21. Foreplay

Sex isn't a chore and sex isn't just a release. Sex is so much more! Take your time to re-explore each other's bodies. Kiss. Touch. Massage. Tease each other until you can barely stand it anymore.

This is the kind of sex that your partner will replay over and over again in their mind. This is the kind of sex that will keep your partner wanting you and only you.

22. Seduce your Partner

They say that your largest sexual organ is your brain. Tease it!

Candles. Dinner. Music. The whole lot. Use this method of mental foreplay to seduce your partner. Add in the element of surprise

35

and take it slow. The anticipation will drive them crazy. Refuse their advances and take the night into your own hands. You are the one seducing. Your partner is the one being seduced.

23.   Wake your Spouse Up with a Favor

Is there any better way than to start the day than with oral sex? Especially if you are not usually the one to initiate sex, this will be an extra special treat.

24.   I'm So Into You

Use your words to affirm your attraction for each other. Pick a time every damn day, and finish this sentence: "Today, I'm into your ___". Sometimes the answer will be hot and steamy. Sometimes it will be funny and playful. Simply, acknowledging what you like about each other is key!

25.   Middle of the Night Sex

Try this. The next time you wake up in the middle of the night, gently spoon your partner and slide your hands on their thighs and start kissing their neck gently until they wake up. Then whisper in their ear what you want to do to them.

This half awake, out of the blue sexual appetite is such a turn on. Your partner will feel extremely desired and the sex will be unlike any sex you've had in a long time. You'll wake up as if it was first date sex...one of those, "Wow, so that happened" feelings.

26.   Quickies

Hey, if you haven't met your quote by the end of the week, it's your duty as a couple to get a quickie in! Make it exciting by meeting at the house during your quick lunch break or popping into your husband's office and pulling down the blinds. These kinds of quickies are sneaky and sexy.

27.   Make up Sex

Some couples are just in the habit of arguing. It's in their nature. Occasional arguments are healthy. Petty arguments are hell.

Never underestimate the power of sex to dissolve an argument. If your argument is about something serious like why you spent your entire paycheck at the casino, you should not use this tactic. But if your argument is about something menial like forgetting to unload the dish washer, and the 2 of you are arguing out of habit...here is a fail-proof tactic to not only stop the argument from escalating but also, to use that aggression towards some hot and steamy sex.

As your partner is scolding you...start undressing. Just start taking your clothes off with a smirk on your face. And then do the same to your partner.

8/10 times, this should work.
The other 2. Well, you tried.

Chapter 4: Respect & Appreciation

Losing respect for your partner can happen quickly through an affair or it can happen over time as your partner changes their lifestyle patterns. Restoring respect and showing appreciation is a "fake it til you make it" kind of path. Respect is a muscle that both of you are going to have to flex over and over again until it grows strong and self-sustaining. And this goes both ways.

You need to feel like your partner respects you.

And you need to be worthy of respect.

This is how we achieve mutual respect. Appreciation follows.

28. Take Responsibility

Let's say you've made a mistake. You were supposed to pick the kids up at 3 and totally forgot. Instead of making excuses and shifting blame, the most respectable thing you can do is say with total sincerity, "I made a mistake".

Don't blanket a mistake with an immediate "I'm sorry" or "My bad". These statements make it seem like you are shrugging off the situation. Instead, stand in that puddle of mistake and let your feet get wet with full responsibility.

First, acknowledge your mistake.

Second, tell you spouse how you'll make sure it doesn't happen again.

Third, apologize for the specific inconvenience.

And be done with it.

The other partner, in turn, must respect and appreciate their partner's willingness to put ego aside and own up to the fault. Then move on.

29.   Be Creepy

Simply watch your spouse. Take a few minutes to observe him or her doing the dishes or solving a crossword puzzle. Watch how their facial impressions change or notice if they still have that cute quirk of singing to themselves unknowingly. Appreciate the little idiosyncrasies that make your spouse special. Notice the weight that they pull and the acts of kindness they do around the house, without ever being asked.

30.   Greet your Partner at the Door

When I asked my father, why he and my mother divorced he told me a story. He said that he had gone to Japan on business for a week and when he came home, smile on his face expecting the family to greet him...no one even got off the couch. He said that this happened every single day. He felt unappreciated, unloved, and alone.

Now, I watch his wife of 15 years enthusiastically jump off the couch and greet him with a big hug and kiss every time he comes home, without failure. He does the same for her. You can literally see the love and appreciation.

Show your partner how loved they are. Put your phone down, get off the couch, and make them feel like they are truly coming home to a place where they are wanted. It's easy, takes 2 seconds, and gives your partner a reason to look forward to coming home.

31.   Leave Notes of Gratitude

Sticky notes are your best friend. Leave little notes around the house, on the steering wheel, in their wallet – that express something your respect or appreciate about him or her.

"Thank you for doing the dishes".
"I admire your dedication to the kids".

"I respect how hard you work every day".

Easy. Effective. Efficient.

32.   Compromise

In the beginning of your relationship, you were so 'go with the flow'. What happened? You'd go to that Italian restaurant even though you were in the mood for Mexican. And you'd watch a horror movie even though it wasn't really your thing.

Now that you're married, your compromises are bigger: babies, houses, jobs, relocation. You must always aim to meet in the middle.

He wants a baby now. She wants a baby in 3 years. Wiggle. Both of you.

33. Respect 'Me Time'

In order to create the best relationship, you need to be your best self. And to do that, you need to take (and give) some 'Me Time'.

What makes you more relaxed? What makes you feel like a badass? Figure it out and do it, with the support of your partner.

Talk about and acknowledge "me time" with each other and for each other. Add your yoga class to the calendar or pick the days where guys night is on the table- but be flexible! Go week by week, if necessary. Maybe your partner wants to hang with their friends for Taco Tuesday this week and play 2 hours of Madden next week on Thursday.

Go with it but don't over-do it! The key is balance and communication and the goal is to feel like each of you have a well-rounded life.

34. Listen Fully

Everyone deserves total focus when they're talking to someone. Especially when that someone is your spouse.

When your partner is talking, put down your damn phone. Is there really any one else on Earth that is more important than your husband or your wife?

Show them the respect they deserve with full eye contact and full attention.

If they start up a conversation while you're in the middle of something that you absolutely cannot put on hold, then make eye contact with your partner and tell them, "I want to fully pay attention to what you're saying, so give me just one second to finish this".

35. No Phones at Dinner

A piggy back onto #34- You have all day to be on your phone. The 'no phones at dinner' rule is an absolute must. Don't even bring them to the table!

Dinner should be sacred. The time where you and your partner come together to catch up and unwind together. Appreciate the little things you get to share by being married to such a wonderfully interesting human being-even if that's just sitting in comfortable silence.

36.   Alone Time

When you first met your partner, all you wanted to do was be alone with them. Once you got comfortable and started blending your regular life together, distractions started seeping in and taking away from that one-on-one appreciation.

It's critical to set aside some alone time where there is nothing more important than your partner. Prioritize your parter and respect your relationship by simply getting a cup of tea and sitting in silence or going for a walk hand-in-hand.

Chapter 5: Finances

In 50% of divorces, couples report finances to be the straw that broke the camels back. Lack of money causes stress. Irresponsible spending by one partner causes distrust. No financial planning creates fear of the future. The two of you must be on the same page when it comes to money, how you spend it, and how you save it.

37.   Create a Budget Together

It's like talking about sex with your parents. For some couples, this can be the most awkward conversation on the planet- but it's a must.

To get on the same page, keep a dossier of your savings, spendings, and monthly income together using apps and websites meant for couples.

Here are a few to check out:
- ✓ Mint App
- ✓ You Need a Budget
- ✓ HoneyDue
- ✓ BetterHaves

38.   Be Honest about your Debt

There is such a thing as financial infidelity. Whether it's debt that you had before you met your partner or it's debt that you've incurred while you've been married, the sooner you come clean, the sooner you can tackle the problem together.

There are 2 reasons why it is so important to be honest about your debt with your partner: 1) because your debt is legally their debt once your married and 2) secrets are poison to marriage.

If you feel like your debt is really bad and you're in way over your head and you're afraid that your partner will leave you because of it- be tactful in how you come clean. Hire a financial advisor and spill the beans together that way you can immediately jump into a solution.

If you decide to tell your partner on your own, don't just tell them the problem, also tell them the solution. For example, don't say "I have $20,000 of debt and I don't know what to do". Instead, say "I have $20,000 of debt and I want to get your opinion on these options I've come up with to dissolve it."

Maybe have a glass of wine ready.
Once this is on the table and the skeletons are out of the closet, you will feel closer to your partner on so many levels.

39. Consider Creating a Combined Bank Account

This is a unifying option best for couples who make around the same salary within $10-20k of each other.

You can either choose to fully combine your finances or to have a separate joint account where you each contribute a specific amount every month. You can use this money as a pure savings account for big ticket items in the future like going on vacation or to use as a bill-paying method for the mortgage or utilities.

This joint account creates a "we" responsibility rather than a "you vs. me" responsibility.

40.   Fun Funds

All of that extra change? It' adds up! Create a piggy bank and fill it with change and $1 bills that will go towards something special that the 2 of you agree on like a new TV or weekend get away.

Treating yourselves together will give you those giddy feelings!

41. Create a Vision Board Together

Visualizing your goals as a couple will actually help you meet them! People swear by vision boards as a key factor in achieving the life and lifestyle they've always dreamed of having.

Here's what you do: get a few old magazine and a big poster board. Spend an afternoon with a couple of beers while clipping out pictures of the things you two want to acquire and the goals you want to achieve together.

Place the board somewhere where both of you can see it, like in the garage where it's right in front of your face every time you come home. You can see the big house, you're reminded of that palm tree vacation, and you hunger for that shiny car.

These shared goals will feed each other's motivation and impact the way you both spend and save money.

Chapter 6: Communication

42. Find your Love Language

A love language is how you express love for another person AND how you receive love from another person.

I might express my love via touch, constantly massaging my partner or rubbing their back. This is how I'm telling my partner "I love you." This also means, I feel most loved when my partner reciprocated by touching me.

However, my partner's love language might be something different. Knowing your partners love language allows you to recognize when they are expressing their feelings for you, and how they will best absorb love from you.

There are 5 Love Languages:

➢ **Words of Affirmation**: Hearing your partners affection through words like "I love you" or "I need you"

➢ **Acts of Service:** When your partner goes out of their way to do something kind for you like cooking dinner or fixing a broken sink

➢ **Physical Touch:** Massages, hand holding, and sex are the channels in which you absorb love

➢ **Quality Time:** Prioritizing time spent with your significant other with no distractions whether at home or on a fun date

➢ **Gifts:** Receiving a gift that lets you know that your partner was thinking about you

To find out your Love Language, take the free quiz at **5LoveLanguages.com**

43.   Work on Conflict Resolution

Some people avoid conflict at all costs and some people beat it like a dead horse. For a marriage to survive inevitable conflict, you need to be able to predict how you AND your partner are going to handle your current conflict, and get into a rhythm of how to sort it out.

First, we must understand why we deal with issues the way we do.

There are so many factors that have contributed to how you deal with conflict. Perhaps your mother always ignored a problem until it went away. Or maybe your father had a healthy way of talking things out. Conflict resolution is a learned habit that has been ingrained in us. But that doesn't mean we can learn to improve upon it – especially when it comes to matching our method of conflict resolution with our partners.

First, share with your partner how your parents and your household dealt with conflict. Compare.

Second, share how you wish they dealt with conflict differently.

Third, make a pact to work towards that ideal resolution scenario.

44.   Argument Oath

You should never want to hurt your partner. Not with words, not with touch, and not with emotional manipulation. But when things get heated, its often easiest to defend yourself with low blows. These low blows may feel good at the time, but can permanently damage the trust in your relationship.

Together, make an list of words and actions that are permanently off limits in a fight; ones that cause your relationship to digress rather than grow. And vow to live by them.

Here are some examples;

- ✓ No name calling
- ✓ Don't use my past infidelity against me
- ✓ No walking away until the problem is resolved
- ✓ Having a 'safe word' that allows an automatic 5-minute breather

- ✓ **Pro Tip:** Bring out the big guns with this rule- No swearing (replace 'fuck' or 'bitch' with 'flapping' or 'bunny' – it usually lightens the situation with a smirk)

45. Don't Harp on Old Issues

Repairing and restoring an old car? You don't keep the broken parts in the trunk do you? That's just going to weigh you down on the highway of life!

Whatever have been the major issues of the past, you both need to agree to LET.IT.GO.

Sit down, write on some pieces of paper the major conflicts, infidelities, and mistakes of the past. Talk about how you acknowledge the damage they did and how you will take action to ensure they are not repeated.

Then crumple them up and burn them. Or throw them in the trash. Or put them in the paper shredder. Whatever.

Once these issues are done, they are never to be brought up to use against the other person in an argument ever again.

46. Honestly Share your Regrets

As a way to start over after a fight or even as a way to start over in the new year, write your regrets down on a piece of paper and burn them.

Sit down together with individual slips of paper and write down something you wish you could take back or something that you're determined to do differently – and then throw them in the fire.

➢ I regret forgetting our anniversary
➢ I regret making you cry
➢ I feel bad for missing movie night

After each slip of paper is thrown in the fire, briefly say how you'll improve upon the situation next time.

- ➢ I'll keep a calendar on my phone
- ➢ I'll choose my words more carefully
- ➢ I'll prioritize our special dates

This is a way to validate your partner's feelings and make them feel heard. This is also a way to dissolve a problem VERY QUICKLY. In fact, don't be afraid to use this tactic in the middle of a fight. Once it's burned, it's done!

47.   5-Year Plan

This doesn't need to be a monthly play by play, but set some goals as to what you want to achieve, where you want to move and if you want to have babies. Highlight those big key factors and make a loose timeline of when you'd like these things to happen.

48.   Tell your Partner What you Need

Most relationships fail because one or both partners aren't having their needs fulfilled. Well, guess what? We can solve that real quick with a simple exercise.

Each of you will get out a piece of paper and draw 2 lines (one vertical and one horizontal) to create 4 boxes. You will title the boxes as follows:

✓ What I've Been Missing
✓ What I Need
✓ What I Want
✓ What I Appreciate Now

As honestly as humanly possible, fill in each box with 3-5 words or statements that meet each quality. Share them with your partner and talk about how you can bring these things to life.

Keep these pieces of paper and hang them on the fridge or the bathroom mirror for a few weeks. Then, save them and revisit them in a month's time. Whatever hasn't yet been met, revisit the topic and try again.

49. Make a Weekly Calendar

A physical calendar! Sit down on Sunday mornings and make a calendar for the next week. Include the 'must do's and the 'want to dos'. By physically creating and looking at a calendar together, you can make sure that you have a balance of responsibility and fun.

50. Make a Monthly or Yearly Calendar

Download a shared calendar app like 'Family Shared Calendar' where you can add in events that are further down the line like anniversaries, work parties, or vacations!

51. Positivity Challenge

Misery loves company! We have a tendency of whirl pooling negative emotions and statements when there is someone to validate them. Then you both end up being big grumps.

Pick 1 day a week where you challenge each other to only saying positive statements. The more you practice this, the more natural it will become.

And remember, positive people attract positive energy. The more positive you become, the more you will become a breath of fresh air to your spouse. No one wants to come home to a rain cloud.

52. Take Personality Quizzes that Matter

There are 2 personality quizzes that every couple should take to understand themselves and their partner on a deeper level.

A) Strengths Based Leadership: While this book was designed for the workplace and team bonding, it is an incredible team builder for your relationship. Discover your strengths and weaknesses, how your partner handles conflict, and how you can work better together.

B) <u>Myers Briggs Personality Test:</u> Do you lead more with your head or your heart? Are you more introverted or extroverted? Use this extremely accurate and scientific personality test to uncover your specific traits and then compare them with your partner to understand how you can work together based on each others' personality needs.

Chapter 7: Acts of Kindness

Acts of kindness are like kerosene for rekindling that flame in your relationship. Surprising someone with a thoughtful deed or generous act will give you a rush of adrenaline. Receiving an unexpected act or gift from your loved one will release serotonin and endorphins in your partner. This feeling can literally become addicting to the both of you.

53.   Slip love notes or funny quotes in your Partner's Pocket

Or purse. Or wallet. Do this 2x a week to build the anticipation and make your partner feel like a kid passing notes in class.

54.   Give your Partner a Surprise Coupon

For no reason at all, slip your partner a "Free Massage" coupon or a "Sexy Time" coupon. These coupons are especially valuable when your schedules are very busy. It will ensure that your partner is getting the attention they need right when they need it.

55.   Make Lunch for Each Other

Do this at least once per week. On Mondays, you make lunch for the both of you. On Wednesdays, it's your partners turn.

Keep it a surprise so your partner has something to look forward to all morning at work. Don't' forget to slip a little love note inside.

56. Wake up to Something Special

Do you usually wake up first? Or did you wake up before your partner on this particular day? Take advantage of this opportunity!

Run to the café and get her favorite coffee or scramble some eggs and serve them to him in breakfast.

57. Iron His Shirt or Her Skirt

These 1950's acts are so novel that they are priceless! Acts of service that are unexpected take barely any effort but have massive impacts with a "Aw you didn't have to do that for me" reaction.

58. Bring Home a Special Treat from the Store

Whether you're picking up a bunch of fresh flowers or grabbing your partner's favorite soda, this small act shows your partner that you were thinking of them and went out of your way to do something nice for them.

59. Have a Bath Waiting

When you partner walks through the door, have them undress and lead them to a luxurious bath with a bottle of wine, candles, and soft music playing. Let them be or sit on the edge of the tub to ask all about their day.

60. Take a Trip Down Memory Lane

Print out a bunch of photos of you and your partner spanning from the beginning of your relationship until now- and don't tell them.

Once a week, tape or hide a photo somewhere where you'll partner will find it.

Sparking these nostalgic memories is a great way to rekindle that relationship that you somehow lost along the way. And it's a super sweet gesture that takes barely any effort at all.

61. Do your Spouse's Chores

Take out the trash. Empty the dishwasher. Do the laundry. These little acts of service take the load off of your partner so when they come home, they can unwind.

62. Give Compliments

Butter your spouse up. There is no such thing as "too many compliments" and these compliments can also be used as positive reinforcement. Did you love the way he kissed you this morning? Tell him how great of a kiss that was. Do you love when she wears that shade of lipstick? Let her know and she's more likely to grab that shade. Your partner feels good and you get more of what you like.

63.   Keep a Journal of Compliments

It's easier to remember the negative things that people say about us rather than the positive ones, isn't it?

Whenever someone says something nice about your partner or gives them a compliment, whether its your family, their friends, or something someone said online, write it down as a quote in a 'Compliment

Journal'. Give this journal to them on a day when they are feeling particularly down.

Not only will this lift your partner's spirits and boost their confidence, but it will also help you see the value in your partner.

64. The Royal Treatment

Ask your spouse to completely clear their schedule on a Sunday and give them the royal treatment. Present them with a card in the morning to let them know how this day is all about them. From breakfast in bed to massages to sex to their favorite movies and snacks. Give little notes and treats throughout the day to keep the surprises coming. Basically, make it a non-birthday birthday.

65. Acts of Kindness Together

Getting involved in charity together is bonding experience that will allow you to witness the softer side of your partner. Write letters to sick children in the hospital at Christmas or make lunches and hand them out to the homeless.

You'll always walk away grateful for the life that the 2 of you have built together. Appreciation is everything.

Chapter 8: Trust & Loyalty

66. Emphasize Unconditional Love

Realize that every relationship is going to come with disagreements and conflict. Understand that butting heads is going to happen when you spend an entire lifetime with another person. Be okay with that.

After, during, before any argument or even when your relationship is sunshine and rainbows, verbally reaffirm to your partner that your love is unconditional, unbreakable, and forever.

That is what marriage is all about.

67.   Forgive and Start Over

Being loyal means that you'll stick by your partner's side no matter what. No matter the mistakes he made or the decisions she choose- it's time to dissolve them and start fresh.

Take whatever issues that currently plague your relationship and choose to forgive them like debt. Truly get rid of that resentment because if you don't, then you can't be 100% loyal because you can't 100% trust.

To do this, divide a piece of paper into 2 sections: What I Want to Forgive You For and What I Want you to Forgive me For.

Take your time to thoughtfully fill these sections out. And do so delicately. The goal isn't to start a fight or dig up arguments that have already been settled. The goal is to address current issues that linger over your relationship, getting in the way of progress.

Take turns reading these to each other. Arguing isn't allowed. If things get heated, hold hands and breathe. Realize that by the end of the exercise, you will have a clean slate on which to rebuild trust.

68.   Set Boundaries and Define Expectations

For couples that deal with jealousy or who have experienced infidelity in the past, it's important to be on the same page moving forward into a healthy relationship built on trust.

Sit down together and create some relationship conditions, just be aware which ones are helpful and which are hurtful.

Here are some examples of healthy conditions vs. harmful conditions...

Unhealthy Relationship -Killing Conditions:

- No talking to other men/women
- Call your partner 5 times a day no matter what
- Setting a curfew for your spouse

Adding such strict constraints in an already strained relationship will almost certainly cause the other person to withdraw. This does not spell out the recipe for L-O-V-E.

Instead, enter into these conditions with trust, compassion, and a little bit of wiggle room.

Healthy Trust-Building Conditions:
- Send me a message at lunch so that I can feel like a part of your day
- Call me on your way home from work
- Introduce me to your coworkers by inviting me for after work beers on occasion

Communication is key; smothering each other is not.

69.   Assume the Best

How many times has jumping to conclusions blown things way out of proportion? Answer: 99% of the time.

Late husband? Give him the benefit of the doubt that traffic was horrid. Wife didn't answer her phone? Assume that it's in the bottom of her purse.

This is called trust.

70.   Work Out Together

Get a gym membership together and start a couple's journey towards a healthy lifestyle and a tight emotional bond.

Allowing your partner to support you during your personal improvement journey builds trust. And witnessing each other overcome physical and mental hurdles promotes mutual respect.

Bonus: Studies show that physiological arousal is hyper-increased between couples that work out together.

71. Don't Bad Mouth your Spouse

Repeat after me: Your partner is not your enemy. Your partner is not your enemy.

You must be careful how harshly you speak of your partner to others. You will be painting a picture of your partner that not only reflects who they are, but also reflects the kind of person you are for being with them.

While we all need someone to vent to, be careful who you choose.

- ✘ Don't vent to your family. Your sister will never forget that your husband called you a bitch when he was drunk.
- ✘ Don't vent to your coworkers. They may never meet your wife and so, can't form their own balanced opinion. Why does their opinion matter? You don't want to be around people who will reinforce this evil stereotype when you bring up your home life.
- ✘ Don't vent to the friends that you and your husband exclusively share.

Instead, pick 1 best friend who is your go-to and speak as if you're being recorded on Dr. Phil. Bring up your points of contention, but don't get nasty. This will only fuel an unnecessary fire.

72. Don't Put yourself in Compromising Situations with the Opposite Sex

It's funny how quickly innocent flirtation can turn into an emotional affair, especially when you're unhappy at home.

If you are truly dedicated to repairing your marriage, become a fiercely loyal soldier to the army that is your marriage and employ tactics to repel advancements or tempting situations by members of the opposite sex.

- **Problem:** You realize that your coworker is hitting on you way too often.

- **Solution:** Talk about your husband more often to make it clear that you are in a happy marriage.

- **Problem:** You find yourself attracted to your wife's best friend.
- **Solution:** Take the time to realistically think about what would really happen if you perused that situation- and how much of a messy dead end you'd wind up in.

73. Share your Secrets

Maybe you've got some serious skeletons in your closet or maybe you're an open book. Either way, try this exercise:

Sit cross-legged on the floor and share 3 secrets under the terms of no judgments in a safe space. This is your chance to reveal that you cheated on your diet last week or that you lost the watch that she gave you for Christmas.

Have a purge of secrets every month! You'll eventually run out of big secrets and have a fun time with the little ones, or you will start to feel comfortable enough to share the big ones you've been too afraid to divulge.

74. Honor your Promises
Did you promise to be home at 8? Be home at 8.

Did you say that you'd take out the trash. Take out the trash.

Did you agree to pick up milk on the way home. Write it on your hand and pick up that milk!

Your word is everything! Big and small.

Chapter 9: Be Playful & Silly

75. Mini Surprise Parties

With no warning, wait for your partner to walk in the door to taco night with Mexican music playing or a game night with Monopoly set up and ready to go along with two glasses of wine. The element of surprise keeps things fun and fresh!

76. Create a Secret Handshake

No explanation needed. Be goofy with your spouse. Use your handshake when it's time to celebrate little wins like saving $5 at the grocery store or when your team scores a point.

77.   Hide and Seek

If you're not physically greeting your partner at the door, greet them with a game. When you hear the garage door open, run and hide – just be sure to leave a 'come and find me' note somewhere where your partner will immediately see it.

This quickly transitions your partner from work mode into play mode. Once he or she gets home, fun time begins!

78.   Spice Up Boring Days

Running errands on a Saturday? Make a challenge to go along with it. Every time you see a woman wearing blue, you kiss. Every time you see a red head, you smack your partner on the butt.

79. Celebrate Random Holidays

It's Arbor Day! Time to go to the park and hug a tree, then sit nearby it's trunk while you have a picnic and involve the tree in Arbor Day conversation.

Don't neglect holidays like National Beer Day or Steak & BJ Day. Any chance to celebrate is a chance to be silly with your best friend.

80. Stupid On-Going Games

Have little inside jokes between the 2 of you that never end. Remember playing "Slug Bug" when you were little? Here are some adult versions of that:

✓ **Drink That Song:** ANYTIME you hear a song playing, you identify the artist and say "drink". Jason Mraz, drink. Phil

Collins, drink. Water, beer, coffee or pretend drink- they must drink whether its morning, afternoon, or evening. No matter where you are, it's a way to always keep the mood light and funny.

✓ **Your Team/ My Team:** See a really weird looking toddler with chubby legs- "your team". See a jacked up Arnold Schwarzenegger look alike "My Team". The idea is that you're constantly building a new colony or team for when the world ends. Just be careful not to pick the sexiest girl in the room for your team...jealousy may ensue.

✓ **Guess the Bill:** When you go out to dinner or shopping at Target, make a small wager. "If you guess within $10, you don't have to pay" or "If you guess within $5, I'll give you a massage".

81. Be Spontaneous

At 10pm on a Thursday, tell your sweetheart to throw on a jacket and some shoes and rush them out the door no matter how silly they look!

Whisk them away to the playground to swing on the swings or the Dairy Queen drive thru and then park and have a sweet little chat about nothing.

82.   Invent a Holiday

....for just the two of you. Like National Flamingo Day where you eat a lot of shrimp and stand on one leg while waiting in line.

Chapter 10: Friends and Family

83.   Blend your Friend Groups

You can't force your friends to like each other, but you can try. Host a game night or a BBQ and bring both of your friends together. To take it 1 step further, suggest a "second date" involving those friends. Be on the look out for shared interested like fishing, music, or pizza (who doesn't love pizza) and suggest another date.

84.   Host a Funny Parties

Your party doesn't have to make sense, it just has to be fun. Host an Ugly Sweater party in February or a White Elephant Party in July.

Make a name for yourselves in your friends and family group as the fun couple. This will become a self-fulfilling prophecy that the two of you will enjoy together.

The more support and love you have from your friends and family, the more likely your marriage is to survive rocky times and be surrounded by encouragement.

85. Invite your Partner to Join in on Your Friends' Traditions

Do you and your friends go bowling together? Do you have wine night? Just ONCE, invite your partner into your world. Obviously, let your friends know first and encourage them to invite their spouses. This 1-time act has multiple benefits:

- ✓ It decreases jealousy by lifting the veil on your "members only" activities
- ✓ The foreign situation lets your partner to see you in a new light.
- ✓ This creates an opportunity for your friends to bond with your partner.

86.   Start Traditions with your Family

Sometimes, there is just no common ground on which to connect with your partner's family. Maybe you're from totally different background with different religions and conflicting opinions on how to raise children. Don't fight those battles in order to find common ground. Instead, build common ground with new traditions – big or small.

- ✓ Have a family game night playing cards and ordering pizza

- ✓ Pick out Christmas Trees Together every Winter
- ✓ Carve Pumpkins at your In-Laws' House (you can carve separate ones at home)
- ✓ Go to the Movies together once a month (no talking necessary!)

87. Hometown Visits

No matter if your partner has been to your hometown before, do it again. But this time, give them the full tour of where you grew up. Show your partner where you had your first kiss, take them to the spot where you used to skip school, show them your high school!

The little kid in you will come alive and shine a totally new light on who you are and how you grew up with your friends and family.

This is the chance for you and your partner to dig a little deeper.

88. Bond Over your Shared Person

Ask your spouse's family and friends to tell you stories about your spouse. You'll learn things you never knew and you'll be tapping into cherished memories that these people will be happy to chat about. The more interest you show in their memories and the more you show interest in your partner, the more these people will begin to see your pure intentions.

89. Include Them

You don't have to throw a massive party in order to include friends and family. Casually invite a couple people over to watch the new episode of Game of Thrones or make an extra portion of spaghetti and tell your sister-in-law to stop by. Just make sure to run this idea past your spouse first!

90.   Create a Family Time Capsule

You may not feel it right away, but your In-Laws are your new family. You'll create memories together and inside jokes together. You'll go through hard times and bad hair cuts, and you'll spend more holidays together than not.

So while it may seem obsolete at the moment, go ahead a create a family time capsule. Pick a box or glass bottle that won't biodegrade in the ground, and ask the important (and even the not-so-important) members of the family to contribute with a sentimental keepsake, a photograph and or a note.

When you dig that baby up in 1 year or 5 years, open it together. This will be a moment that you really feel like a family.

91. Mail Handwritten Letters to your In-Laws

For no special reason at all. Receiving hand-written letters and post cards is so "old school" that it's quite a novel gesture. Send printed photos or invitations to a causal Sunday night dinner. This cuts down on the obligation to call them on the phone or visit their house every week, but makes them feel included.

92. Ask for Advice

Is your spouse's mom a nurse? Ask what is the best way to take care of your sprained ankle (even though you could Google it). Is your partner's best friend an electrician? Ask him if he'd teach you how to turn your living room light into a dimming light.

The point isn't the end result, the point is that you are showing interest in that person and indirectly complimenting their expertise.

93. Give it Time

Some people take longer than other to warm up. Maybe your husband's mom seems like a real bitch. But guess what? You're stuck with her. Always take the higher ground and extend warm greetings and invitations. The same goes for sisters, brothers, and friends.

Keep being yourself. Keep being kind. And be patient. They'll come around. Even if you've made big mistakes in the past, trust that they will come around as long as you keep that door open.

Chapter 11: Date Ideas

Courtship should never end! Once you stop dating, you just become roommates. Bring back the romance- for both of you – with date night at least once per week. It doesn't have to be fancy or expensive (although, those kinds of dates should be sprinkled in throughout the year). The date night only needs to signify that you are willing to prioritize your partner.

94. Double Date

Double dates can actually improve your relationship.

Seeing that your partner is funny and likeable in a group dynamic is attractive.

Watching your partner interact on a social level is sexy. And sitting alongside your partner in a public situation strengthens the feeling of being part of a team.

When your relationship and your partner receive approval, you tend to value that relationship even more. In fact, studies show that all of these double dating outcomes breed passion in a relationship. It's a big win all together.

95.   The Ultimate Movie Night
Here is a reoccurring date night that allows you two to share interests and cuddles at the same time.

Pick a movie together, get the heaviest comforter you can find, take the pillows off the bed, and snuggle up on the couch with some popcorn. Oh, and turn those phones off!

Or for an even more exciting movie night, take turns planning the entire night from the movie to the delivery. Keep it a surprise.

Consider designating an official movie night and do it every week without fail. Traditions are glue for marriages.

96.   Mystery Date

Twice a month, you and your partner will have a mystery date, taking turns to plan it.

You'll write a clue or a series of clues in a poem to a certain location. Be sure to include the time. Slip this clue inside of a manila envelope that your partner is only allowed to open once they leave the house. Your partner will solve the clue and be treated to a fun-filled dinner or activity totally planned by you!

97.   Scavenger Hunt

Create a sentimental scavenger hunt for your partner where you've hidden clues a head of time.

For example: "You can find your next clue where I make the stew." And leave a clue in the crock pot!

The clues should eventually lead outside of the house and to a destination like a restaurant or movie theater.

Leave clues with the receptionist at your doctor's office or the cashier at your local gas station. Involving shared places and commonly known people will make your partner feel unbelievably special and loved.

98. Sporting Event

Has he never been to a hockey game? Take him! Has she never seen a basketball game live? Change her perspective! The more out of the norm that your date is, the more exciting it will be – even if the event isn't your partner's "typical" idea of fun.

99. Go Ice Skating

If you're having trouble with physical affection, ice skating can fix that problem real quick. Because, as we all know, holding hands while ice skating is mandatory!

This is the kind of date that is enjoyable from beginning to end as your get bundled up with a cozy scarf and some warm mittens. Maybe even buy your partner a new beanie to set the mood.

Once you hit the ice, it's impossible not to have fun. You don't have to be a pro for this to go well. In fact, falling a few times is adorable and only leads to more opportunities for physical contact.

100. Game Night

The most causal, laid back night you can have with a friend is game night. Pure fun with no pressure or expectations. In fact, friend zone each other for the entire night.

Once a week, pick a board game like Scrabble or Sorry and order some Chinese food and just chill out. The rule is no touching or sexy shenanigans until game night is totally over. This is a platonic bonding experience that will bring you closer and allow you to learn about each other.

Plus, being stuck together for hours and hours at a time is a great way to bond, learn a bit about each other, and get outside of your comfort zone with your best friend by your side.

Pro Tip: Pack the night before to get extra excited and take the stress of the day.

Bonus: The Best Bonding Date Ever

101. Road Trip

Whether it's a daytime road trip to the seaside or a 3-day road trip full of gas station food and motels, get out of town and be tourists together!

Buy silly hats, use fake names, create some music playlists, and play road trip games like 20 Questions to pass the time and have some laughs!

The Beautiful Conclusion

Everything I'm going to tell you right now is true...which is why you've heard before:

- ✓ Marriage takes work
- ✓ You need to choose your partner ever day
- ✓ There are going to be good years and bad years
- ✓ You. Get. The. Point.

But something no one has ever told you?

A real marriage changes, evolves, and grows. It looks different every year and feels different every 5. It's not supposed to be the same in the end as it was in the beginning...because **you** will not be the same. You'll grow, too. Don't fight that change. Roll with it.

Let this Marriage Check List change your marriage! Rip apart the things that aren't working and patch up the things that are. Create, mold, and give life to something beautiful between the one whom you **choose** to love.

Plan to fall in love with your partner over and over again. Actively and deliberately. Keep this book tucked away on your shelf (or on your futuristic Kindle machine) and revisit these rules in times of trouble and in times of monotony. For the more you practice and weave these methods into your marriage, the stronger and more colorful it will become.

Made in the USA
Las Vegas, NV
17 November 2022

59636212R00066